Naaman's dreadful secret

Story by Penny Frank
Illustrated by Tony Morris

THE LION
STORY BIBLE

23

OXFORD · BATAVIA · SYDNEY

The Bible tells us how God chose the nation of Israel to be his special people. He made them a promise that he would always love and care for them. But they must obey him.

This story is about a Syrian man called Naaman and how God showed his power through the prophet Elisha in the land of Israel.

You can find the story in your Bible, in the second book of Kings, chapter 5.

Copyright © 1987 Lion Publishing

Published by
Lion Publishing plc
Sandy Lane West, Littlemore, Oxford, England
ISBN 0 85648 748 1
ISBN 0 7459 1768 2 (paperback)
Lion Publishing Corporation
1705 Hubbard Avenue, Batavia, Illinois 60510, USA
ISBN 0 85648 748 1
Albatross Books Pty Ltd
PO Box 320, Sutherland, NSW 2232, Australia
ISBN 0 86760 532 4
ISBN 0 7324 0088 0 (paperback)

First edition 1987, reprinted 1988
Paperback edition 1989

British Library Cataloguing in Publication Data

Frank, Penny
Naaman's dreadful secret. – (The Lion Story Bible; 23
1. Naaman – Juvenile literature
I. Title   II. Morris, Tony
222'.540924   BS580.N2

ISBN 0-85648-748-1
ISBN 0-7459-1768-2 (paperback)

Printed in Yugoslavia

Library of Congress Cataloging in Publication Data

Frank, Penny.
Naaman's dreadful secret.
(The Lion Story Bible; 23)
1. Naaman, the Syrian – Juvenile
literature. 2. Bible. O.T. – Biography –
Juvenile literature. 3. Bible stories,
English – O.T. Kings, 2nd. [1. Naaman,
the Syrian. 2. Elijah, the Prophet.
3. Bible stories – O.T.] I. Morris, Tony,
ill. II. Title. III. Series: Frank, Penny.
Lion Story Bible; 23.
BS580.N2F73 1987   222'.5409505
86-2863
ISBN 0-85648-748-1
ISBN 0-7459-1768 2 (paperback)

Naaman was a great general in the
Syrian army. The Syrians were fighting
the Israelites.

When the king of Syria saw how
many prisoners Naaman brought back
from Israel, he was very pleased with
him. He let him take one little girl home,
as a present for his wife.

Naaman was a great soldier, but he had
a dreadful secret. None of his friends
knew. None of his soldiers knew. Not
even the king knew.

Only Naaman's wife knew the secret.
Naaman was very ill. He had a terrible
skin disease. It was getting worse and
worse all the time.

Poor Naaman! He tried to cover it up.
But he knew that soon people would see
the marks on his face and hands.

Naaman's wife was very sad. She loved
Naaman. She tried to pretend that
nothing was wrong. She tried to look
happy and pretty.

She knew that when their friends found out they would send Naaman away. He would not be an important man any more.

There was nothing that could make him better.

One morning Naaman's wife started to cry. The little servant girl Naaman had brought from Israel saw her crying.

'Please don't cry,' she said. 'You will make your face red. Look, I have put out your best yellow dress to wear. Do cheer up.'

But Naaman's wife kept on crying.

'Whatever is the matter?' asked the little servant girl.

'General Naaman has a terrible skin disease,' his wife said. 'When everyone finds out they won't want us as friends. Naaman will be sent away.'

The little girl thought for a while. Then she said, 'I know a man in Israel who could help. His name is Elisha. He is a prophet of our God. Our God could make Naaman well again.'

Naaman's wife ran to tell her husband.

Naaman had to tell the king of Syria his secret so that he could go to Israel. He took some men with him, and a letter for the king of Israel.

When Naaman got to Israel the king was frightened.

'Is the king of Syria trying to start another battle?' he said. 'How can I make Naaman well? I'm not God.'

Just then there came a message from the prophet Elisha.

'Don't be frightened,' the message said. 'Just send Naaman to me.'

13

The king was pleased.

'You need to visit the prophet Elisha, not me,' he told Naaman.

All the servants bowed low to Naaman as he went from the palace.

'Oh dear, let's hope Elisha helps him,' they said. 'We don't want another battle.'

15

Naaman's chariot drew up outside Elisha's house. But no one invited him in.

Elisha's servant came out with a message.

'Elisha says you must wash in the River Jordan seven times and you'll be well.'

Naaman was furious.

'Who does this Elisha think he is? I thought he would come out himself and pray to his God. I'm not washing in a muddy river in Israel!'

Naaman's servants said, 'Why not? You might as well try what the prophet said. It's such an easy thing to do. Even a child can wash himself.'

They went on to the River Jordan.

Naaman went down to wash in the river. The men waited for him on the bank. They counted for him.

'One, two, three times.' They were glad they did not have to go in the water with him.

The water was brown and cold.
Naaman's feet slipped on the rough
stones. He felt like giving up.

'Four, five, six times,' shouted the men
on the bank. 'Don't stop now. Elisha said
seven times.'

When Naaman came out of the water
the seventh time he looked down at his
skin. It was smooth and just like new.
There were no marks anywhere.

Naaman was well. He was very
happy.

Naaman and his servants rushed back to tell Elisha. They thanked God all the way there.

Naaman told Elisha, 'Now I know that the God of Israel is the only true God.'

Naaman decided he was going to worship the God of the Israelites. He could not wait to get back to Syria to tell his wife, so that she could worship him, too.

23

The Lion Story Bible is made up of 52 individual stories for young readers, building up an understanding of the Bible as one story — God's story — a story for all time and all people.

The Old Testament section (numbers 1–30) tells the story of a great nation — God's chosen people, the Israelites — and God's love and care for them through good times and bad. The stories are about people who knew and trusted God. From this nation came one special person, Jesus Christ, sent by God to save all people everywhere.

The story of General Naaman comes from the Old Testament history book, 2 Kings, chapter 5. It shows God's love and care for everyone, not just his own special people.

Because of their kindness to their little Israelite servant girl, General Naaman and his wife learned where to go for help when disaster struck.

And because in the end he was not too proud to do just as God's prophet Elisha told him, Naaman was completely healed — and discovered for himself the true God.

The next story in this series, number 24: *Enemies all around*, takes place in the southern kingdom of Judah. Can anything save King Hezekiah and his people from the terrible armies of Assyria?